jams &
conserves

THE AUSTRALIAN
Women's Weekly

Looking at all the glorious fruits we now have available to buy, the prospect of getting out the jam pan is so much more exciting. There is still an abundance of fruit in accordance with its natural season, but there are also great deals on fruit throughout the year. Making jams, jellies or conserves is such a simple process and when you taste the wonderful results... you will only wonder why you didn't try sooner. Take special note of how to sterilise the jars thoroughly and you will be bottling all year round!

Pamela Clark

Food Director

contents

tips & techniques

Here are some tried-and-tested tips that will give you success every time; they are simple techniques that work perfectly, and it's important to read them before you start to cook. If you follow these procedures, your jams, jellies and marmalades will be a triumph – tasty, delicious and simple to prepare.

JAMS AND CONSERVES

Jam is based on either one fruit or several different fruits. A conserve is a preserve made from whole or large pieces of fruit. It is made in the same way as jam.

fruit for jams and conserves

Fruit should be as freshly picked as possible, and slightly under-ripe; at this stage the pectin (the setting agent in preserves) content is at its highest. For best results, make small amounts of jam at a time. The shorter cooking time will give better results in flavour, texture and appearance. As a guide, avoid using more than 2kg fruit for any jam recipe.

The most suitable fruits for jam making are those which have a good balance of acid and pectin; however, lemon juice can be added to fruits low in acid or pectin to improve their setting properties

- fruits with good balance of acid and pectin are: grapes, crab apples, currants, quinces, sour gooseberries, grapefruit, lemons, limes, sour apples, sour guavas, sour oranges, sour plums.
- fruits high in pectin and low in acid are: sweet apples, sweet guavas, sweet quinces. When making jam or jelly from these fruits, you need to add 2 tablespoons lemon juice to each 1kg fruit.
- fruits low in pectin and high in acid are: apricots, pineapples, rhubarb, sour peaches. When making jam from these fruits, you need to add 2 tablespoons lemon juice to each 1kg fruit.
- Fruits low in acid and pectin and not suitable for making jam without adding other fruits or juice are: pears, melons, sweet peaches, cherries and most berries including strawberries, raspberries and blueberries.

equipment used for preserves

Use large wide-topped stainless steel or enamel saucepans or boilers; do not use copper or unsealed cast iron pans because the acid in the preserve will damage the metal, and colour and flavour the ingredients.

Aluminium pans should not be used as they can taint the flavour of the jam.

jam making

There is a basic method for making jam if you can't find a suitable recipe. This will always work provided the fruit is at its peak for jam making and the pectin/acid content is balanced.

1 Wash fruit well, cut away any bruised or damaged parts. Chop or slice fruit, reserve seeds; these provide extra pectin for setting. They can be soaked separately in half a cup of water, then the seeds strained out and discarded. The gelatinous liquid left is added to the fruit. Seeds can also be tied in a muslin bag and cooked with the fruit; the bag is discarded later. Citrus rind needs overnight soaking to soften; in this case fruit is cooked in the soaking liquid – see marmalades, page 8.

2 Place fruit in pan; fruit layer should not be more than about 3cm deep. Add enough water to barely cover fruit, cover pan, bring to boil over high heat, reduce heat, simmer gently. It is important that fruit be simmered until it is as tender as required; once the sugar is added, further cooking will not tenderise the fruit any more. This can take from about 10 minutes for soft fruit such as berries, or up to 1½ hours for tough citrus rinds.

3 Once the fruit or rind is tender, measure fruit mixture in a measuring

To test if jam has jelled

Dip a wooden spoon into the mixture, hold spoon up above mixture and tilt the bowl of the spoon towards you; as mixture cooks and thickens, the drops will fall more heavily from the spoon. When it is ready, 2 or 3 drops will roll down the edge of the spoon and join together in a heavy mass. When this happens, remove jam or jelly from heat to stop further cooking. Drop a teaspoon of mixture onto a saucer which has been chilled in freezer for a few minutes, return saucer to freezer until jam or jelly is at room or serving temperature but not frozen.

- Jam which has pieces of fruit in it should have formed a skin which wrinkles when pushed with the finger.
- Jam which is pulpy in texture should be of a spreadable consistency.
- Jelly should be a firm mass on the saucer. If mixture does not jell, return to the heat, boil rapidly until mixture will jell when tested; this may take only a few more minutes.

NOTE Jams and jellies will reach jelling point at 105°C to 106°C (220°F to 222°F). Any sugar thermometer can be used.

cup or jug, allow 1 cup sugar to each cup of fruit mixture.

4 Return fruit mixture to pan; it should not be more than about 3cm deep; bring to boil. Add sugar to pan: the mixture at this stage should not be more than about 5cm deep.

5 Stir fruit mixture over high heat to dissolve sugar quickly. Sugar must be dissolved before mixture boils or jam may crystallise. Use pastry brush dipped in water to brush down sides of pan and wooden spoon to remove every single grain of sugar.

6 Once sugar is dissolved, boil the jam as rapidly as possible for time given in recipe or until the mixture is thick or will jell. This can take from 10 minutes up to an hour. Do not stir jam after sugar has dissolved, but use a wooden spoon to check that the jam is not sticking on the base of the pan, particularly towards the end of cooking time When jam has cooked for the required time, start testing to see if jam has jelled.

7 When jam is at jelling stage, skim surface, if necessary. If jam contains pieces of fruit, let stand for 5 to 10 minutes before bottling. This allows the mixture to cool slightly and the fruit to disperse more evenly (marmalade usually requires the full 10 minutes standing time). Jams made from pulpy fruit should be bottled immediately.

8 Pour jam into hot sterilised jars right to the top of the jar, jam will shrink on cooling.

9 Seal jars while hot. Label jam and store in a cool dark place. If jam has been cooked and sealed correctly, it will keep for at least 12 months. Once opened, store in refrigerator.

To test for pectin content

Place 1 teaspoon of the strained fruit liquid in a glass, add 3 teaspoons methylated spirits; stir mixture gently with a teaspoon.

• If mixture forms a fairly solid single jelly-like clot, the fruit liquid is high in pectin; in this case measure the liquid and use 1 cup sugar to each cup of liquid. (This jelly will set quickly, without long cooking time; there will be little evaporation of liquid, giving a good yield of jelly for the amount of fruit used.)

• If several smaller clots of jelly form, the jelly is not high in pectin; use ¾ cup sugar to each cup fruit liquid.

• If pectin test fails to produce any clots, or gives a mass of tiny clots, it will then be necessary to add some fruit juice naturally rich in pectin, usually 2 tablespoons fresh strained lemon juice to each 1kg fruit; add this after the sugar is dissolved.

If jam has not set

This is due to an imbalance of pectin and acid; or insufficient evaporation in the cooking process. Lemon juice can be added and jam re-boiled until it will jell when tested. However, if jam has darkened in colour and has a caramel taste (which happens when sugar is overcooked) it cannot be re-boiled. If the flavour is still palatable, commercial pectin (available in powdered or liquid form from health food stores and supermarkets) will set the jam; follow the manufacturer's directions.

JELLIES

A good jelly should be clear and translucent, firm enough to hold its own shape, but soft enough to quiver when cut with a spoon. The strained juice from the cooked fruit is combined with sugar, then cooked to a point at which it will set when cold.

basic steps in jelly making

1 Wash fruit thoroughly, cut away any bruised or damaged parts. Chop fruit roughly, stems, seeds, skin and all.
2 Place prepared fruit in pan: fruit layer should not be more than 3cm deep. Add enough water to barely cover fruit, so fruit just begins to float.
3 Cover pan, bring to boil over high heat, reduce heat, simmer gently, covered, until fruit is tender and just beginning to become pulpy. The time varies, depending on type and

ripeness of fruit, between 30 minutes and 1 hour.
4 Strain fruit mixture through a fine cloth. There are several easy methods of doing this:
• A cone-shaped jelly bag can be bought from specialist kitchen stores; have it thoroughly damp before use. Place a large bowl under the bag. Pour the fruit and liquid into the bag; do not push or force the fruit through, as this will cause the jelly to cloud. Cover loosely with a tea towel to protect the fruit from dust and insects, leave liquid to drip through cloth; this will take up to 12 hours.
• If you don't have a jelly bag, make one by turning a chair or stool upside down on a table; tie corners of a square of damp fine cloth securely to the legs of the chair, leave cloth loose enough to dip in the centre.
• If you are in a hurry, and not too concerned about the clarity of the jelly, strain the fruit through a large strainer or colander suspended over a bowl. Pour fruit mixture into strainer, press fruit with a wooden spoon to extract as much liquid as possible; discard the pulp. To remove any remaining pulp from liquid, place a clean piece of damp fine cloth inside a strainer over a bowl, pour the liquid into cloth and let it to drip through; do not force the liquid through the cloth.
5 Measure the liquid in a measuring cup or jug; determine how much sugar is required, according to

recipes (generally ¾ cup or 1 cup sugar to each cup of liquid, depending on the fruit). If not following a recipe, the pectin test on page 6 will indicate the amount of sugar required.

6 Return fruit liquid to pan, there should not be more than 3cm covering base of pan.

7 Bring to the boil over high heat, add sugar, stir without boiling until sugar is dissolved. Brush all sugar grains from sides of pan and wooden spoon; use a pastry brush dipped in water to do this. Heat must be kept high to dissolve sugar quickly for best results.

8 When mixture comes to the boil, leave on high heat. Boil as rapidly as possible, uncovered, without stirring, for minimum time suggested in recipe. (These times are only a guide; constant watching and testing is necessary.) High heat must be maintained without allowing the mixture to boil over.

10 When mixture jells, allow bubbles to subside, lift off any scum from the surface. Using a jug, pour jelly in a slow stream down the side of hot sterilised jars. Work quickly and do not stir or move the jelly too much with the jug, or jelly will not be clear.

11 Fill jars right to the top; jelly will shrink slightly on cooling.

12 Seal jars while hot. It will take at least 12 hours for jelly to become cold. Store in a cool dark place. Jelly should keep for 12 months. Once a jar is opened, keep refrigerated.

If jelly has not set

This is due to a lack of pectin and/or acid. Re-boiling will cause jelly to lose clarity and texture; the addition of commercial pectin will also spoil its appearance, but will at least make the jelly set; follow the manufacturer's instructions.

MARMALADES

Marmalade is a clear jelly preserve with small pieces of rind or fruit suspended in it. They are made from citrus fruits, or a combination of fruits, one or two being citrus. Many marmalade recipes suggest fruit to be soaked overnight. This extracts pectin and begins to soften the rind. If time does not permit overnight soaking, simply cook for longer than recipe instructs, but be careful not to evaporate too much liquid or the balance of ingredients will be upset. Some recipes require the seeds to be soaked and then boiled with the fruit (see tips for jams and conserves). Fruit, along with the water in which it was soaked, is cooked, covered, over a low heat until the rind is tender; this takes between 30 minutes and 1½ hours, depending on thickness and toughness of rind. Once sugar is added, further cooking will not tenderise the rind, so be sure it is tender before the sugar is added. Follow detailed instructions for jam making when making marmalades; fruit can also be minced, blanched or chopped in a food processor.

Jars

Jars must be glass, without chips or cracks; and should be sterilised. As a general rule, hot preserves go into hot sterilised jars, cold preserves go into cold sterilised jars. Jars must always be dry. Tea-towels and hands must be clean when handling jars. Unclean jars can cause deterioration in preserves.

To sterilise jars

in dishwasher: use rinse cycle and hottest temperature, do not use detergent.
without a dishwasher: method 1: place clean jars lying down in pan, cover completely with cold water, cover pan, bring to boil and boil, covered, for 20 minutes; carefully remove jars from water (thick rubber gloves and tongs are useful for this): drain well, stand right way up on wooden board. The heat from the jars will quickly evaporate any water remaining in the jars.
method 2: wash jars well in hot soapy water, rinse thoroughly in hot water. Stand jars right way up on board in cold oven (do not allow jars to touch); turn oven to very low, leave for 30 minutes, remove from oven.

To seal jars

Preserve must be correctly sealed while it is still hot in order to prevent deterioration. Ordinary metal lids are not suitable; the acid content of the preserve will corrode the lids and the contents will be inedible. Special lined and treated or lacquered lids are suitable for sealing. Plastic screw-top lids give a good seal (plastic snap-on lids are not airtight enough). Plastic lids must be well washed, rinsed and dried. Some older preserving jars have glass lids; these can be sterilised by either of the above methods. Do not use aluminium foil, cellophane or paper covers for preserves; foil will be corroded by the acid in the preserves and paper and cellophane are not airtight enough for long term keeping. Wipe sealed jars clean, label and date.

To store jars

Store preserves in a cool, airy, dark, dry place (light can cause deterioration) until required. Once opened, all preserves must be stored, covered, in the refrigerator.

Jams

strawberry jam

1.5kg strawberries, hulled
125ml fresh lemon juice
1.25kg sugar

1 Combine strawberries, juice and sugar in large saucepan; stir over heat, without boiling, until sugar dissolves.
2 Bring to a boil; simmer, uncovered, without stirring, for about 20 minutes or until jam jells when tested.
3 Pour hot jam into hot sterilised jars; seal while hot.

makes about 1.25 litres

raspberry jam

1½kg raspberries
2 tablespoons lemon juice
1½kg sugar
1 tablespoon Crème de Framboises liqueur

1 Combine berries and juice in large saucepan, stir gently over low heat for 5 minutes or until raspberries are soft.
2 Stir in sugar over heat, without boiling, until sugar is dissolved. Bring to boil, boil, uncovered, without stirring, for 10 minutes or until jam jells when tested. Stir in liqueur.
3 Pour hot jam into hot sterilised jars; seal while hot.

makes about 1.5 litres

three berry jam

500g strawberries hulled
500g blackberries
500g raspberries
1.25kg sugar
60ml lemon juice

1 Combine berries in large saucepan, stir gently over low heat
for 5 minutes. Measure fruit mixture, allow 1 cup sugar to each cup
of fruit mixture. Return fruit mixture and sugar to pan; stir in juice.
Stir over heat, without boiling, until sugar is dissolved.
2 Bring to boil and boil, uncovered, without stirring, for about
20 minutes or until jam jells when tested.
3 Pour hot jam into hot sterilised jars; seal while hot.

makes about 1.25 litres

frozen berry jam

4 large oranges (880g)
1kg frozen berries, thawed
1kg sugar
2 tablespoons Crème de Framboises liqueur
6 tablespoons slivered almonds

1 Thickly peel oranges, cut into segments; reserve any juices, discard seeds. Combine berries, oranges, reserved juice and sugar in large saucepan, stir gently over low heat without boiling until sugar is dissolved.
2 Bring to boil, boil, uncovered without stirring for about 30 minutes or until jam jells when tested.
3 Stir in liqueur and almonds; stand 10 minutes before pouring into hot sterilised jars; seal while hot.

makes about 1 litre
tip You can use any berries in this recipe.

any berry liqueur jam

1kg berries
1kg sugar
250ml lemon juice
3 tablespoons Cointreau

1 Combine berries, sugar and juice in a large saucepan, stir over heat, without boiling, until sugar is dissolved.
2 Bring to boil; boil, uncovered, without stirring, for about 25 minutes or until jam jells when tested.
3 Stir in liqueur, pour into hot sterilised jars; seal while hot.

makes about 1.25 litres
tip You can use any berries in this recipe. Try strawberries, raspberries, blackberries, blueberries, loganberries…

brandied cherry jam

900g frozen pitted cherries
180ml water
60ml lemon juice
125ml cherry brandy
880g white sugar, approximately

1 Combine cherries, the water and juice in large saucepan; bring to the boil. Reduce heat; simmer, covered, about 10 minutes or until cherries are soft. Stir in brandy.
2 Measure fruit mixture; allow 165g sugar for each cup of mixture. Return mixture and sugar to pan; stir over heat, without boiling, until sugar dissolves. Boil, uncovered, about 40 minutes or until jam sets when tested on a cold saucer.
3 Pour into hot sterilised jars; seal immediately.

makes 1 litre

red, black & blue jam

400g frozen raspberries
300g frozen blackberries
300g frozen blueberries
500ml water
125ml fresh lemon juice
880g sugar, approximately

1 Combine berries with the water and juice in large saucepan; bring to a boil. Reduce heat; simmer, uncovered, 20 minutes.
2 Add sugar; stir over heat, without boiling, until sugar issolves.
3 Boil, uncovered, stirring occasionally, about 15 minutes or until jam jells when tested.
4 Pour hot jam into hot sterilised jars; seal while hot.

makes about 1.5 litres
tips Choose fruit in season when it is at its most plentiful and cheap or use a good crop from your own garden. Fresh berries give the best results, but frozen fruits are a fairly good substitute.

apricot jam

25 medium apricots (1kg)
375ml water
1.25kg sugar, approximately

1 Halve apricots and break open a quarter of the stones, remove kernels; lightly crush kernels, add to fruit. Combine apricots, kernels and water in large saucepan, bring to boil, simmer, covered, for about 15 minutes or until apricots are soft.
2 Measure the fruit mixture, allow 1 cup sugar to each cup of fruit mixture.
3 Return fruit mixture and sugar to pan, stir over heat, without boiling, until sugar is dissolved. Bring to boil; boil, uncovered, without stirring, for about 15 minutes or until jam jells when tested.
4 Pour into hot sterilised jars; seal while hot.

makes about 1.25 litres

dried apricot jam

500g dried apricots, chopped coarsely
1.25 litres water
1kg sugar
60ml fresh lemon juice

1 Combine apricots and the water in large bowl; cover, stand overnight.
2 Transfer apricot mixture with sugar and juice to large saucepan; stir over heat, without boiling, until sugar dissolves. Boil, uncovered, stirring occasionally, about 25 minutes or until jam jells when tested.
3 Pour hot jam into hot sterilised jars; seal while hot.

makes about 1.5 litres

apricot & apple jam

18 medium apricots (750g)
5 large apples (1kg), peeled, chopped
750ml water
1kg sugar, approximately

1   Halve apricots and discard stones. Combine apricots, apples and water in large saucepan.
2   Bring to boil, simmer, covered, for 30 minutes.
3   Measure fruit mixture, allow ¾ cup sugar to each cup of fruit mixture. Return fruit mixture and sugar to pan, stir over heat, without boiling, until sugar is dissolved. Bring to boil, boil, uncovered, without stirring, for 30 minutes or until jam jells when tested.
4   Pour hot jam into hot sterilised jars; seal while hot.

makes about 1.5 litres

dried peach & apple jam

400g coarsely chopped dried peaches
150g dried apples, chopped coarsely
1.25 litres water
1kg sugar
60ml fresh lemon juice

1   Combine fruit and the water in large bowl; cover, stand overnight.
2   Transfer fruit mixture with sugar and juice to large saucepan; stir over heat, without boiling, until sugar dissolves. Boil, uncovered, stirring occasionally, about 25 minutes or until jam jells when tested. Remove pan from heat.
3   Pour hot jam into hot sterilised jars; seal while hot.

makes about 1.5 litres

peach & raspberry jam

2 medium peaches (300g), peeled, chopped
500g raspberries
330g sugar
2 teaspoons grated lemon rind
60ml water
2 tablespoons port

1   Combine peaches, raspberries, sugar, rind and water in large saucepan. Stir over heat, without boiling, until sugar is dissolved.
2   Bring to boil; boil, uncovered, without stirring, for about 15 minutes or until until jam jells when tested. Stir in port.
3   Pour hot jam into hot sterilised jars; seal while hot.

makes about 750ml

nectarine jam

8 large nectarines (1.5kg)
125ml lemon juice
440g sugar, approximately

1   Halve nectarines, discard stones, finely chop nectarines. Combine nectarines and juice in large saucepan. Bring to boil, simmer, covered, for about 20 minutes or until nectarines are soft.
2   Measure fruit mixture, allow ¾ cup sugar to each cup of fruit mixture. Return fruit mixture and sugar to pan, stir over heat, without boiling, until sugar is dissolved. Bring to boil, boil, uncovered, without stirring, for 10 minutes or until jam jells when tested.
3   Pour hot jam into hot sterilised jars; seal while hot.

makes about 750ml

dried spiced fruit jam

150g chopped dried apples
150g chopped dried peaches
500g chopped dried figs
1 litre water
1 teaspoon grated lemon rind
2 cinnamon sticks
1.5 litres water, extra
125ml lemon juice
2.75kg sugar

1 Combine dried fruit, water, rind and cinnamon in large bowl, cover stand overnight.
2 Combine undrained fruit mixture, extra water and juice in large saucepan. Bring to boil, simmer, covered, for about
15 minutes or until fruit is soft.
3 Measure fruit mixture, allow 1 cup sugar to each cup of
fruit mixture. Return fruit mixture and sugar to pan, stir over heat, without boiling, until sugar is dissolved.
4 Bring to boil, boil, uncovered, without stirring, for about
50 minutes or until jam jells when tested. Discard cinnamon sticks. Pour jam into hot sterilised jars; seal while hot.

makes about 2.75 litres

fruit salad jam

1 medium grapefruit (390g)
1 large orange (220g)
4 medium limes (340g)
500ml water
1 small pineapple (500g), peeled, cored, chopped coarsely
4 medium apples (500g), peeled, chopped
1 litre water extra
770g sugar approximately
125ml passionfruit pulp (approximately 6 passionfruit)

1 Remove rind from grapefruit, orange and limes, cut rind into very thin strips. Combine rind and water in bowl. Remove and discard pith from grapefruit, orange and segments, reserving any juice. Reserve seeds, tie in a piece of muslin, add to bowl with rind, cover; stand overnight.
2 Combine undrained rind mixture, segments and juice, pineapple, apples and extra water in large saucepan. Bring to boil, simmer, covered, 1 hour.
3 Measure fruit mixture, allow ¾ cup sugar to each cup fruit mixture.
4 Return fruit mixture and sugar to pan, stir over heat without boiling, until sugar is dissolved. Bring to boil; boil, uncovered, without stirring, for about 20 minutes or until jam jells when tested.
5 Discard bag of seeds; stir in passionfruit. Stand 10 minutes, stirring occasionally. Pour into hot sterilised jars; seal when hot.

makes about 1.5 litres

spiced fig & apple jam

2 large granny smith apples (500g), peeled,
   chopped finely
500ml water
16 medium fresh figs (1kg), chopped coarsely
125ml orange juice
1.1kg caster sugar, approximately
2 tablespoons finely grated orange rind
1 teaspoon ground cinnamon
pinch ground cloves

1 Bring apple and water to a boil in large saucepan. Reduce heat; simmer, covered, about 20 minutes or until apples are soft. Add figs and juice; simmer, covered, 10 minutes.
2 Measure fruit mixture; allow ¾ cup (165g) sugar for each cup of mixture.
3 Return fruit and sugar to pan with remaining ingredients; stir over heat, without boiling, until sugar dissolves. Boil, uncovered, 45 minutes or until jam jells when tested.
4 Pour into hot sterilised jars; seal while hot.

makes 2 litres
tip Finely grate the rind from the oranges before juicing them.

apple & red fruit jam

2 medium lemons (280g)
1 medium apple (150g)
60ml fresh lemon juice
300g frozen raspberries, thawed
250g strawberries, halved
440g sugar

1   Peel rind thinly from lemons, avoiding white pith. Cut rind into very thin strips. Peel and core apple, cut into thin wedges.
2   Combine rind, apple, juice, berries and sugar in large saucepan; stir over heat, without boiling, until sugar dissolves.
3   Boil, uncovered, stirring occasionally, about 15 minutes or until jam jells when tested.
4   Pour hot jam into hot sterilised jars; seal while hot.

makes about 750ml

apple & blackberry jam

4 large apples (800g)
800g blackberries
125ml water
1kg sugar, approximately

1   Peel, core and finely chop apples. Combine apples, berries and water in large saucepan. Bring to boil, simmer, covered, for 30 minutes until fruit is soft. Measure fruit mixture, allow ¾ cup sugar to each cup of fruit mixture. Return fruit mixture and sugar to pan, stir over heat, without boiling, until sugar is dissolved.
2   Bring to boil, boil, uncovered, without stirring, for 15 minutes or until jam jells when tested.
3   Pour hot jam into hot sterilised jars; seal while hot.

makes about 1.5 litres

apple & ginger jam

2 medium lemons (360g)
6 large apples (1.25kg), peeled, sliced
1.25 litres water
50g fresh ginger, peeled, sliced
1.25kg sugar, approx
120g stem ginger, chopped

1 Using vegetable peeler, thinly remove rind from 1 lemon;
squeeze juice from lemons – to get 60ml of juice.
2 Combine apples, water and juice in large saucepan.
Tie rind and fresh ginger in piece of muslin, add bag to pan.
Bring apple mixture to boil, simmer, covered, for 30 minutes;
discard muslin bag.
3 Measure fruit mixture, allow 1 cup sugar to each cup of fruit
mixture.
4 Return fruit mixture and sugar to pan, stir over heat, without
boiling, until sugar is dissolved. Bring to boil, boil, uncovered,
without stirring, for about 15 minutes or until jam jells when tested.
Stir in stem ginger; stand 5 minutes.
5 Pour into hot sterilised jars; seal while hot.

makes about 1.25 litres

rhubarb & ginger jam

1.5kg rhubarb, chopped
250ml water
2 tablespoons lemon juice
5cm piece fresh ginger, peeled
1.25kg caster sugar
6 tablespoons finely chopped stem ginger

1 Combine rhubarb, water, juice and fresh ginger in large saucepan. Bring to boil, simmer, covered for 1 hour. Remove and discard ginger.
2 Measure fruit mixture, allow ¾ cup sugar to each cup of fruit mixture. Return fruit mixture and sugar to pan. Stir over heat, without boiling, until sugar is dissolved. Stir in stem ginger.
3 Bring to boil, boil, uncovered, without stirring, for 15 minutes or until jam jells when tested.
4 Pour hot jam into hot sterilised jars; seal while hot.

makes about 1.5 litres

plum jam

18 medium red plums (2kg)
1 litre water
80ml fresh lemon juice
1.3kg sugar

1 Cut plums into quarters, remove stones. Combine plums and the water in large saucepan; bring to a boil. Reduce heat; simmer, covered, 1 hour.
2 Add juice and sugar; stir over heat, without boiling, until sugar dissolves.
3 Boil, uncovered, stirring occasionally, for about 20 minutes or until jam jells when tested.
4 Pour hot jam into hot sterilised jars; seal while hot.

makes about 2 litres

cumquat & cointreau jam

1kg cumquats
1.5 litres water
1.5kg sugar, approximately
60ml Cointreau

1 Cut cumquats into quarters, remove and reserve seeds. Put seeds and 250ml of the water in small bowl; cover, set aside. Combine fruit with remaining water in large bowl. Stand both fruit mixture and seeds, separately, overnight.

2 Drain seeds over small bowl; reserve liquid, discard seeds. Combine fruit mixture and seed liquid in large saucepan; bring to a boil. Reduce heat; simmer, covered, about 45 minutes or until rind is tender.

3 Measure fruit mixture, allow 1 cup sugar to each cup of fruit mixture. Return to pan with sugar; stir over heat, without boiling, until sugar dissolves. Boil, uncovered, stirring occasionally, about 25 minutes or until jam jells when tested. Stand 5 minutes; stir in liqueur. Pour hot jam into hot sterilised jars; seal while hot.

makes about 1.5 litres

blueberry & passionfruit jam

750g blueberries
750ml water
550g sugar, approximately
60ml fresh lemon juice
2 tablespoons passionfruit pulp (about 2 passionfruit)

1 Combine blueberries and water in large pan; bring to a boil. Reduce heat; simmer, uncovered, about 20 minutes or until blueberries are tender.
2 Measure fruit mixture, allow ¾ cup sugar to each cup of fruit mixture. Return fruit mixture with sugar and juice to pan; stir over heat, without boiling, until sugar dissolves. Boil, uncovered, stirring occasionally, about 20 minutes or until jam jells when tested.
3 Stir in passionfruit pulp; stand 5 minutes.
4 Pour hot jam into hot sterilised jars; seal while hot.

makes about 750ml
tip You will need approximately 2 passionfruit for this recipe.

quince jam

9 medium quinces (2kg)
2 litres water
1 tablespoon grated lemon rind
165ml lemon juice
1.25kg sugar

1 Peel and quarter quinces; remove and discard cores. Chop quinces into small pieces, combine with water, rind and juice in a large saucepan. Bring to boil, simmer, covered, 1 hour.
2 Stir in sugar, stir over heat, without boiling, until sugar is dissolved. Bring to boil, boil, uncovered, without stirring, for about 30 minutes or until jam jells when tested. Pour hot jam into hot sterilised jars; seal while hot.

makes about 2.5 litres

pineapple jam

2 medium pineapples (2kg), peeled, cored, chopped coarsely
1.25 litres water
165ml fresh lemon juice
1.5kg sugar

1 Combine pineapples, the water and juice in large saucepan; bring to a boil. Reduce heat; simmer, covered, about 1 hour or until pineapple is soft.
2 Stir in sugar; stir over heat, without boiling, until sugar is dissolved. Boil, uncovered, without stirring, about 30 minutes or until jam jells when tested.
3 Pour hot jam into hot sterilised jars; seal while hot.

makes about 1.5 litres

papaya & pineapple jam

2 medium firm papayas (2kg)
1 medium pineapple (1.25kg)
100g finely chopped stem ginger
500ml fresh lemon juice
2kg sugar

1 Quarter, deseed and peel papayas; chop into 2cm pieces. Peel pineapple, remove core; chop pineapple into 2cm pieces. Combine papaya, pineapple, ginger and juice in large saucepan; bring to a boil. Reduce heat; simmer, uncovered, 5 minutes.
2 Add sugar; stir over heat, without boiling, until sugar dissolves. Boil, uncovered, stirring occasionally, about 30 minutes or until jam jells when tested; stand 5 minutes.
3 Pour hot jam into hot sterilised jars; seal while hot.

makes about 3 litres

tropical fruit salad jam

250g dried apricots	125ml fresh orange juice
500ml water	60ml passionfruit pulp
250ml can crushed pineapple in syrup	660g sugar
	300g sliced bananas

1 Combine apricots and the water in medium bowl; cover, stand 3 hours or overnight.

2 Combine undrained apricots with undrained pineapple in large pan; simmer, covered, 15 minutes. Add juice and passionfruit pulp, bring to a boil; reduce heat, simmer, covered, 10 minutes.

3 Add sugar; stir over heat, without boiling, until sugar issolves.

4 Add banana; boil, uncovered, stirring occasionally, about 20 minutes or until jam jells when tested. Stand 5 minutes.

5 Pour hot jam into hot sterilised jars; seal while hot.

makes about 1.5 litres

rose petal jam

100g dark red rose petals (approximately 20 pesticide-free petals)	330g sugar
	1 tablespoon lemon juice
750ml water	2½ tablespoons Certo apple pectin

1 Trim white or yellow sections from petals. Combine petals and water in large saucepan, bring to boil, simmer, covered, for 30 minutes. Strain, reserve liquid.

2 Combine reserved liquid, sugar, juice and pectin in pan. Stir over heat, without boiling, until sugar is dissolved. Bring to boil, boil, uncovered, without stirring, for about 10 minutes or until jam jells when tested. Stir in petals.

4 Pour hot jam into hot sterilised jars; seal while hot.

makes about 500ml

kiwi fruit jam

12 large kiwi fruit (1.2kg)
2 tablespoons Certo apple pectin
2 tablespoons water
2 tablespoons fresh lemon juice
440g sugar
green food colouring, optional

1 Cut peeled kiwi fruit into eighths, discard seeds and core. Blend or process the water, juice and 1 tablespoon of the sugar until smooth. Add kiwi fruit; process until chopped coarsely.
2 Combine kiwi fruit mixture with remaining sugar in large saucepan; stir over heat, without boiling, until sugar dissolves.
3 Boil, uncovered, stirring occasionally, 10 minutes. Stir in pectin; boil for 30 seconds or until jam jells when tested.
4 Tint with food colouring, if desired.
5 Pour hot jam into hot sterilised jars; seal while hot.

makes about 625ml
tip The green food colouring in this recipe gives the jam a lush, green colour. If you prefer not to use it, the finished jam will taste just as delicious!

apricot & passionfruit jam

500g dried apricots, halved
60ml fresh lemon juice
500ml water
880g caster sugar
125ml passionfruit pulp

1 Combine apricots, juice and the water in large microwave-safe bowl; cook, uncovered, on HIGH (100%) 15 minutes, stirring once during cooking. Add sugar; stir until sugar dissolves.
2 Cook, uncovered, on HIGH (100%) about 10 minutes or until jam jells when tested, stirring three times during cooking.
3 Add passionfruit pulp; stand 2 minutes, stir jam to distribute seeds. Pour hot jam into hot sterilised jars; seal while hot.

makes about 1.25 litres
tip You will need about six passionfruit for this recipe.

rhubarb berry jam

440g coarsely chopped rhubarb
500g fresh or frozen blackberries
1 teaspoon finely grated orange rind
1 tablespoon fresh orange juice
1 tablespoon fresh lemon juice
385g caster sugar

1 Combine rhubarb, berries, rind and juices in large microwave-safe bowl; cook, uncovered, on HIGH (100%) 10 minutes, stirring once during cooking. Add sugar; stir until sugar dissolves.
2 Cook, uncovered, on HIGH (100%) about 20 minutes or until jam jells when tested, stirring three times during cooking. Pour hot jam into hot sterilised jars; seal while hot.

makes about 750ml

tomato jam

Microwave
jams

4 medium tomatoes (750g), peeled
1 small apple (130g), peeled,
    grated coarsely
65g finely chopped stem ginger
60ml fresh lemon juice
440g caster sugar

1   Coarsely chop tomatoes, combine with apple and ginger in large microwave-safe bowl; cook, uncovered, on HIGH (100%) about 15 minutes or until mixture is pulpy. Add juice and sugar; stir until sugar dissolves.
2   Cook, uncovered, on HIGH (100%) about 20 minutes or until jam jells when tested, stirring three times during cooking. Pour hot jam into hot sterilised jars; seal while hot.

makes about 1 litre

The colour and flavour of jams cooked in a microwave oven is excellent, and these mouth-watering recipes on these pages will attest to that. When microwaving jams, always use a large, shallow microwave-safe bowl and remember to follow the golden rule: check the preserve often during cooking time. These recipes have been tested in a 900-watt microwave oven.

strawberry liqueur conserve

250g strawberries
220g sugar
2 teaspoons finely grated lemon rind
2 tablespoons fresh lemon juice
liqueur
500g strawberries
110g sugar
125ml gin

1 Place strawberries in medium saucepan with sugar, rind, juice and reserved strawberries from liqueur. Stir gently over heat, without boiling, until sugar dissolves.
2 Boil, uncovered, gently stirring, occasionally, about 10 minutes or until conserve sets to a spreading consistency when tested.
3 Pour hot conserve into hot sterilised jars; seal while hot.
liqueur Combine strawberries in jar with sugar and gin; cover, stand for 3 days. Shake jar gently several times a day. Remove strawberries from liquid; reserve strawberries. (Liquid can be used as a dessert sauce or served as a liqueur).

makes about 500ml

strawberry conserve

1.5kg strawberries, hulled
1.1kg white sugar
250ml lemon juice

1 Gently heat berries in large saucepan, covered, for 5 minutes to extract juice from berries. Transfer berries with slotted spoon to large bowl; reserve.

2 Add sugar and lemon juice to pan, stir over heat, without boiling, until sugar dissolves; bring to the boil. Boil, uncovered, without stirring, 20 minutes. Add reserved berries to pan; simmer, uncovered, without stirring, 25 minutes or until jam jells when tested.

3 Pour jam into hot sterilised jars; seal while hot.

makes 1.5 litres

apricot rum conserve

500g dried apricots, chopped
1 litre water
80ml fresh lemon juice
1kg sugar
2 tablespoons dark rum

1 Combine apricots, the water and juice in large saucepan;
bring to a boil. Reduce heat; simmer, covered, about 30 minutes
or until apricots are tender.
2 Add sugar; stir over heat, without boiling, until sugar dissolves.
Boil, uncovered, stirring occasionally, about 15 minutes or until
conserve jells when tested. Stir in rum.
3 Pour hot conserve into hot sterilised jars; seal while hot.

makes about 1.5 litres

fig & ginger conserve

12 medium figs (1kg), chopped
125ml orange juice
2 tablespoons lemon juice
1 tablespoon sweet sherry
1½ tablespoons grated fresh ginger
440g sugar

1 Combine figs, juices, sherry and ginger in large saucepan. Bring
to boil, simmer, covered, about 20 minutes or until figs are soft.
2 Stir in sugar; stir over heat, without boiling, until is sugar dissolved.
Bring to boil, boil, uncovered, without stirring, for about 20 minutes
or until conserve jells when tested.
4 Pour hot conserve into hot sterilised jars; seal while hot.

makes about 750ml

golden plum conserve

14 medium golden plums (1kg)
250ml water
2 tablespoons lemon juice
60ml orange juice
1.25kg sugar, approximately
240g sultanas
3 tablespoons stem ginger, chopped
1 tablespoon rum

1 Halve plums, discard stones, cut plums into quarters.
2 Combine plums, water and juices in large saucepan. Bring to boil, simmer, covered, for about 10 minutes or until plums are soft.
3 Measure fruit mixture, allow 1 cup sugar to each cup of fruit mixture. Return fruit mixture and sugar to pan, stir over heat, without boiling, until sugar is dissolved. Stir in sultanas and ginger. Bring to boil, boil, uncovered, for about 20 minutes, without stirring, or until conserve jells when tested. Stir in rum.
4 Pour hot conserve into hot sterilised jars; seal while hot.

makes about 1.25 litres

apricot & mint conserve

38 medium apricots (1.5kg)
3 medium lemons (540g)
125ml water
1.5kg sugar
1 tablespoon white vinegar
2 tablespoons chopped fresh mint
2 tablespoons grated fresh ginger

1 Halve apricots, remove stones. Break open a quarter of the stones, remove kernels, lightly crush kernels, reserve.
2 Squeeze lemons, reserve juice and seeds.
3 Tie reserved kernels and seeds in muslin bag. Combine apricots, water and muslin bag in large saucepan. Bring to boil, simmer, covered, for about 25 minutes, stirring occasionally, or until mixture is pulpy. Discard muslin bag
4 Stir in sugar and reserved juice, stir over heat, without boiling, until sugar is dissolved. Stir in vinegar, mint and ginger.
5 Bring to boil, simmer, uncovered, without stirring, for about 45 minutes or until conserve jells when tested.
6 Pour into hot sterilised jars; seal while hot.

makes about 2 litres

rhubarb & carrot conserve

4 medium carrots (500g), chopped
500g rhubarb, chopped
1 teaspoon grated lemon rind
2 tablespoons lemon juice

1 litre water
1kg sugar
3 tablespoons stem ginger,
    chopped

1   Combine carrots, rhubarb, rind, juice and water in large saucepan.
Bring to boil, simmer, covered, for about 15 minutes, or until carrots are soft.
2   Stir in sugar and ginger, stir over heat, without boiling, until sugar is
dissolved. Bring to boil, boil, uncovered, without stirring, for about
15 minutes or until conserve jells when tested.
3   Pour hot conserve into hot sterilised jars; seal while hot.

makes about 2 litres

rhubarb & orange conserve

2kg rhubarb, chopped
1.5kg sugar
4 large oranges (880g)
2 medium limes (170g)

40g currants
3 tablespoons pine nuts
2 tablespoons Cointreau

1   Combine rhubarb and sugar in large saucepan. Peel oranges and limes
thinly using vegetable peeler; cut rind into thin strips. Squeeze juice from
oranges (you will need 125ml juice); squeeze juice from limes (you will need
2 tablespoons juice).
2   Stir juices and rinds into pan, stir over heat, without boiling, until sugar is
dissolved. Bring to boil, boil, uncovered, without stirring, for about 45 minutes
or until conserve jells when tested.
3   Stir in currants, nuts and liqueur; stand; 10 minutes before pouring into
hot sterilised jars; seal while hot.

makes about 2 litres

Jellies

apple jelly

1kg apples chopped
1.5 litres water
1kg sugar, approximately

1 Combine apples and water in large saucepan. Bring to boil, simmer, covered, for 1 hour.
2 Strain mixture through fine cloth. Allow liquid to drip through cloth slowly, do not squeeze cloth; discard pulp.
3 Measure liquid, pour into large saucepan. Add correct amount of sugar (according to pectin test, page 6) to each cup of liquid, stir over heat, without boiling, until sugar is dissolved. Bring to boil, boil, uncovered, for 15 minutes or until jelly sets when tested.
4 Pour hot jelly into hot sterilised jars; seal while hot.

makes about 750ml
tips Use any good quality fresh eating apples in these recipes – Granny Smiths are nice and crunchy, but the most important things is to use apples as fresh as possible. Those from cold storage may not give such good results.

black grape & port jelly

1kg black grapes
2 medium lemons (280g), chopped coarsely
1 litre water
125ml port
1kg sugar, approximately

1 Combine grapes, lemon (including rind and seeds) and the water in large saucepan; bring to a boil. Reduce heat; simmer, covered, 45 minutes. Stir in port, crush grapes in pan using a potato masher.
2 Simmer, covered, 45 minutes. Strain mixture through large piece of damp muslin into large bowl; allow mixture to drip through cloth for several hours or overnight. Do not squeeze or press the mixture through the cloth as this will result in cloudy jelly.
3 Measure the strained liquid, discard pulp. Allow the correct amount of sugar (according to pectin test, page 6) to each cup of liquid. Return liquid with sugar to clean large saucepan; stir over heat, without boiling, until sugar dissolves. Boil, uncovered, without stirring, about 15 minutes or until jelly sets when tested.
4 Pour hot jelly into hot sterilised jars; seal while hot.

makes about 1 litre

grape jelly

1.5kg black grapes
165ml water
80ml lemon juice
500g sugar, approximately
3 tablespoons Certo apple pectin

1   Using scissors, snip grapes from main stems, leaving small
stems attached to grapes. Crush grapes in large pan, stir in water
and juice.
2   Bring to boil, simmer, covered, for 10 minutes or until fruit is pulpy.
Strain mixture through fine cloth. Allow mixture to drip through
cloth slowly, do not squeeze cloth, discard pulp. Measure liquid,
pour into large saucepan. Add correct amount of sugar
(according to pectin test, page 6) to each cup of liquid. Stir over
heat, without boiling, until sugar is dissolved. Bring to boil, stir in
pectin, boil, uncovered, for 5 minutes or until jelly sets when tested.
4   Pour hot jelly into hot sterilised jars; seal while hot.

makes about 750ml

apple honey sauternes jelly

5 large apples (1kg), chopped coarsely
2 tablespoons fresh lemon juice
500ml water
250ml sauternes
60ml honey
660g sugar, approximately

1 Combine apple (plus seeds and cores), juice, water, wine and honey in large saucepan; bring to a boil. Reduce heat; simmer, covered, 1 hour.

2 Strain mixture through large piece of damp muslin into large bowl; allow mixture to drip through cloth for several hours or overnight. Do not squeeze or press the mixture through the cloth as this will result in cloudy jelly.

3 Measure the strained liquid, discard pulp. Allow the correct amount of sugar (according to pectin test, page 6) to each cup of liquid. Return liquid with sugar to clean large saucepan; stir over heat, without boiling, until sugar dissolves. Boil, uncovered, without stirring, about 10 minutes or until jelly sets when tested.

4 Pour hot jelly into hot sterilised jars; seal while hot.

makes about 750ml

raspberry jelly

2kg raspberries
1kg sugar, approximately
1 tablespoon lemon juice

1 Place raspberries in large pan, stir over low heat for 10 minutes
or until pulpy. Strain mixture through fine cloth. Allow liquid to drip
through cloth slowly, do not squeeze cloth; discard pulp.
2 Measure liquid, pour into large saucepan. Add correct amount
of sugar (according to pectin test, page 6) to each cup of liquid,
add juice, stir over heat, without boiling, until sugar is dissolved.
3 Bring to boil, boil, uncovered, for 10 minutes or until jelly sets
when tested.
4 Pour hot jelly into hot sterilised jars; seal while hot.

makes about 1 litre

redcurrant & raspberry jelly

600g redcurrants
800g raspberries
250ml water
440g sugar, approximately

1 Combine fruit and water in large saucepan. Bring to boil
simmer, covered, for 25 minutes or until fruit is soft.
2 Strain mixture through fine cloth. Allow liquid to drip through
cloth slowly, do not squeeze cloth; discard pulp.
3 Measure liquid, pour into large saucepan. Add correct amount
of sugar (according to pectin test, page 6) to each cup of liquid,
stir over heat, without boiling, until sugar is dissolved. Bring to boil,
boil, uncovered, for 10 minutes or until jelly sets when tested.
4 Pour hot jelly into hot sterilised jars; seal while hot.

makes about 500ml

clementine jelly

1kg clementines, chopped
1 medium lemon, chopped
2.5 litres water
550g sugar, approximately

1 Combine clementines, lemon and water in large saucepan. Bring to boil, simmer, covered, for 1 hour or until fruit is soft and pulpy. Strain mixture through fine cloth. Allow liquid to drip through cloth slowly, do not squeeze cloth; discard pulp.
2 Measure liquid, pour into large saucepan. Add correct amount of sugar (according to pectin test, page 6) to each cup of liquid, stir over heat, without boiling, until sugar is dissolved.
3 Bring to boil, boil, uncovered, for 5 minutes or until jelly sets when tested. Pour hot jelly into hot sterilised jars; seal while hot.

makes about 500ml
tip Any member of the clementine family is suitable for this recipe – try tangerines, mandarins or satsumas.

quince jelly

1.75kg quinces, chopped
1.75 litres water
1.25kg sugar, approximately
125ml lemon juice

1 Combine quinces and water in large saucepan, bring to boil, simmer, covered, for 1 hour or until quinces are soft.
2 Strain mixture through fine cloth. Allow liquid to drip through cloth slowly, do not squeeze cloth; discard pulp.
3 Measure liquid, pour into large saucepan. Add correct amount of sugar (according to pectin test, page 6) to each cup of liquid, add juice, stir over heat, without boiling, until sugar is dissolved.
4 Bring to boil, boil, uncovered, for 25 minutes or until jelly sets when tested. Pour hot jelly into hot sterilised jars; seal while hot.

makes about 1 litre
tips Quinces are large yellow-skinned fragrant fruit with crunchy cream flesh that, when slow-cooked, turns a deep ruby-red colour. The good thing about making jelly is that you do minimal preparation, which is especially useful with quinces, as they are notoriously hard to peel. Just chop the unpeeled fruit and use the lot – skins, cores and alll.

pistachio quince paste

50g chopped pistachios, toasted
4 lemon-flavoured tea bags
625ml boiling water
1.4kg quinces
125ml lemon juice
1 teaspoon ground cloves
880g caster sugar

1 Grease a 23cm round sandwich pan; sprinkle chopped pistachios over base.
2 Combine tea bags and water in large bowl, stand 30 minutes. Discard tea bags.
3 Peel, core and roughly chop quince; combine with tea, juice and cloves in large pan. Simmer, covered, about 45 minutes or until quince is tender. Blend or process quince mixture, in batches, until smooth.
4 Return quince mixture to same pan with sugar, stir over heat, without boiling, until sugar is dissolved. Simmer, uncovered, stirring frequently, about 30 minutes or until very thick and darker in colour. Gently pour quince mixture into prepared pan; stand at room temperature until set.

makes about 1 litre

fig & quince paste

Membrillo

1kg quinces
160g dried figs, chopped
1 cinnamon stick
880g caster sugar, approximately
60ml lemon juice

1   Peel, core and quarter quinces; combine in large saucepan
with figs, cinnamon and enough water to cover, bring to the boil.
Simmer, covered, about 1 hour or until most liquid is absorbed.
2   Discard cinnamon; process mixture until pulpy. Measure mixture
into same pan. Add 1 cup caster sugar to every 1 cup pulp; stir in
juice, stir until sugar dissolves.
3   Cook, over very low heat, about 2 hours or until mixture leaves
side of pan. Pour into oiled and lined deep 20cm-round cake tin.
Stand at room temperature overnight until set. Serve as part of a
cheese platter.

makes 1 litre

Membrillo (the Spanish for
quince) is a delicious
quince jelly originating in
Spain, where it is a popular
accompaniment to
manchego cheese.

orange passionfruit butter

5 eggs, beaten, strained
165g caster sugar
2 passionfruit
3 teaspoons grated orange rind
125ml orange juice
60ml water
125g butter, chopped

1 Combine eggs and sugar in top half of double saucepan or in heatproof bowl. Stir in passionfruit pulp and remaining ingredients.
2 Stir mixture over simmering water until mixture thickly coats the back of a wooden spoon.
3 Pour into hot sterilised jars; seal when cold.

makes about 750ml

All butter recipes will keep for several weeks in the refrigerator. Presented in attractive jars, butters and spreads make welcome gifts at Christmas.

lemon & lime butter

180g butter, chopped
500ml caster sugar
125ml lemon juice
1 teaspoon grated lime rind
80ml lime juice
4 eggs, beaten, strained

1   Combine all ingredients in top half of double saucepan or in heatproof bowl. Stir over simmering water until mixture thickly coats the back of a wooden spoon.
2   Pour into hot sterilised jars; seal when cold.

makes about 750ml

citrus spread

2 large oranges (440g)
1 medium lemon (180g)
1 medium lime (85g)
1 litre water
1.75kg sugar

1   Blend or process unpeeled, chopped fruit, with seeds, with the water in batches until finely chopped.
2   Transfer mixture to large saucepan, add sugar, stir over heat, without boiling, until sugar is dissolved. Bring to boil, boil, uncovered, without stirring, for about 15 minutes or until mixture will spread when cold. Pour into hot sterilised jars; seal when cold.

makes about 2 litres

lemon ginger butter

6 egg yolks
165g caster sugar
1 teaspoon grated lemon rind
250ml lemon juice
1½ teaspoons ground ginger
3 tablespoons stem ginger, finely chopped
180g butter, chopped

1   Combine egg yolks and sugar in top half of double saucepan or in heatproof bowl, stir in rind, juice, gingers and butter.
2   Stir over simmering water until mixture thickly coats the back of a wooden spoon.
3   Pour into hot sterilised jars; seal when cold.

makes about 500ml
tip Always buy unwaxed lemons for jam and marmalade making. If you can't buy unwaxed, then a good scrub with a stiff brush will remove most traces of wax.

plum butter

7 medium plums (500g), stones removed, chopped
60ml lemon juice
4 eggs, beaten, strained
165g caster sugar
125g butter, chopped

1   Combine plums and juice in large saucepan. Bring to boil, simmer, covered, for about 20 minutes or until plums are soft. Push plum mixture through sieve. Discard pulp.
2   Combine eggs and sugar in top half of double saucepan or in heatproof bowl; stir in plum mixture and butter. Stir over simmering water until mixture thickly coats the back of a wooden spoon.
3   Pour mixture into hot sterilised jars; seal when cold.

makes about 750ml

nutty plum spread

14 medium plums (1kg)
440g brown sugar
60ml orange juice
60ml lemon juice
6 tablespoons chopped pecans or walnuts
6 tablespoons chopped stem ginger

1   Halve plums, discard stones, chop plums roughly. Combine plums, sugar and juices in large saucepan. Stir over heat, without boiling, until sugar is dissolved, bring to boil, simmer, uncovered, stirring occasionally, for about 20 minutes or until mixture is thick and will spread when cold. Stir in nuts and ginger.
2   Pour into hot sterilised jars; seal when cold.

makes about 750ml

cherry lemon spread

1.25kg cherries, pitted
125ml water
440g sugar, approximately
½ teaspoon grated lemon rind
2 tablespoons lemon juice

1 Combine cherries and water in large saucepan, bring to boil,
simmer, covered, for about 15 minutes or until cherries are soft.
Push cherries through sieve, discard skins. Measure cherry mixture;
allow 1 cup sugar to each cup of cherry mixture. Return cherry
mixture and sugar to pan, add rind and juice. Stir over heat,
without boiling, until sugar is dissolved.
2 Bring to boil, boil, uncovered, for about 15 minutes or until
mixture will spread when cold.
3 Pour into hot sterilised jars; seal when cold.

makes about 500ml

banana spread

3 medium (500g) ripe bananas
80ml lemon juice
125g butter, chopped
4 egg yolks

1 Blend or process bananas until smooth.
2 Combine bananas, juice, butter and egg yolks in top half of a
double saucepan or in a heatproof bowl. Stir over simmering
water until mixture thickly coats the back of a wooden spoon.
3 Spoon hot spread into hot sterilised jars; seal while hot.

makes about 500ml

raspberry red spread

250g raspberries
440g caster sugar
50g cornflour
2 eggs, beaten, strained
2 tablespoons grated lemon rind
165ml lemon juice
80g butter, chopped

1 Blend or process berries until smooth.
2 Combine berries and remaining ingredients in saucepan,
stir over heat until mixture boils and thickens.
3 Pour mixture into hold sterilised jars; seal while hot.

makes about 750ml

seville orange marmalade

6 small Seville oranges (1kg)
2 litres water
2kg sugar, approximately

1 Slice unpeeled oranges finely, reserve seeds. Combine oranges and the water in bowl, cover; stand overnight. Place seeds in a cup, barely cover with water, cover; stand overnight.

2 Transfer fruit mixture to large saucepan, bring to boil, simmer, covered for about 45 minutes or until rind is soft.

3 Measure fruit mixture, allow 1 cup sugar to each cup of fruit mixture. Return fruit and sugar to pan, stir in liquid from seeds; discard seeds. Stir over heat, without boiling, until sugar is dissolved.

4 Bring to boil, boil, uncovered, without stirring. for 20 minutes or until marmalade jells when tested.

5 Pour hot marmalade into hot sterilised jars; seal while hot.

makes about 1.75 litres
tip For a delicious variation, stir in 60ml whisky before bottling the marmalade.

three-fruit marmalade

4 large oranges (1.2kg)
3 medium lemons (420g)
4 large limes (400g)
1.25 litres water
1.6kg white sugar, approximately

1 Peel all fruit thinly; cut rind into thin strips. Remove pith from all fruit; reserve half, discard remaining pith. Chop flesh coarsely, reserve seeds.

2 Combine flesh and rind in large bowl with the water. Tie reserved pith and seeds in muslin; add to bowl. Stand at room temperature overnight.

3 Place fruit mixture and muslin bag in large pan; bring to the boil. Reduce heat; simmer, covered, 25 minutes or until rind is soft. Discard bag.

4 Measure fruit mixture; allow 1 cup (220g) sugar for each cup of mixture. Return mixture and sugar to pan; stir over heat, without boiling, until sugar dissolves. Boil, uncovered, about 40 minutes or until marmalade gels when tested.

5 Pour into hot sterilised jars; seal immediately.

makes 1.75 litres
tip Lime rind takes the longest to cook, so it's the one to check. It needs to be very soft.

cumquat marmalade

1kg cumquats
1.25 litres water

2 tablespoons lemon juice
1.25kg sugar

1 Cut fruit in half, remove seeds; tie seeds in a piece of muslin. Slice fruit thinly, combine fruit, muslin bag and water in large bowl, cover, stand overnight.
2 Transfer mixture to large saucepan, stir in juice. Bring to boil, simmer, covered for about 30 minutes or until cumquat skins are soft; discard bag.
3 Add sugar, stir over heat, without boiling, until sugar is dissolved. Bring to boil, boil, uncovered, without stirring, for 20 minutes or until marmalade jells when tested.
4 Pour hot marmalade into hot sterilised jars; seal while hot.

makes about 1.75 litres

tangy lemon marmalade

6 medium lemons (1kg)
1.75 litres water
1kg sugar

1 Cut rind thinly from lemons; slice finely. Cut pith from lemons; chop roughly, reserve. Cut flesh into thin slices; reserve seeds. Combine flesh and rind in large bowl with water. Tie reserved pith and seeds in piece of muslin; add to bowl, cover, stand overnight.
2 Transfer mixture to large saucepan, bring to boil, simmer, covered, for 40 minutes or until rind is soft; discard muslin bag. Add sugar, stir over heat, without boiling, until sugar dissolves.
3 Bring to boil, boil, uncovered, without stirring, for 30 minutes or until marmalade jells when tested.
4 Pour hot marmalade into hot sterilised jars; seal while hot.

makes about 1.5 litres

thick-cut orange, grapefruit & ginger marmalade

2 medium grapefruit (850g)
2 medium oranges (480g)
1.75 litres water
1.5kg sugar, approximately
2 tablespoons grated fresh ginger

1 Cut fruit in half, remove and discard seeds. Cut fruit into quarters, then cut quarters into thick slices. Combine fruit with the water in large bowl; cover, refrigerate overnight.

2 Transfer fruit mixture to large saucepan; bring to a boil. Reduce heat; simmer, covered, about 45 minutes or until fruit is soft.

3 Measure fruit mixture, allow 1 cup sugar to each cup of fruit mixture. Return fruit mixture with sugar and ginger to pan; stir over heat, without boiling, until sugar dissolves. Boil, uncovered, stirring occasionally, about 40 minutes or until marmalade jells when tested.

4 Pour hot marmalade into hot sterilised jars; seal while hot.

makes about 1.75 litres

lime ginger marmalade

12 medium limes (1kg)
1.5 litres water
1.75kg sugar, approximately

1 Slice unpeeled limes thinly, remove and discard seeds. Combine limes in large bowl with the water; cover, stand overnight.
2 Transfer lime mixture to large saucepan; bring to a boil. Reduce heat; simmer, covered, about 1 hour or until rind is tender.
3 Measure fruit mixture, allow 1 cup sugar to each cup of fruit mixture. Return fruit mixture with sugar to pan; stir over heat, without boiling, until sugar dissolves. Boil, uncovered, stirring occasionally, about 20 minutes or until marmalade jells when tested. Stir in ginger.
4 Pour hot marmalade into hot sterilised jars; seal while hot.

makes about 2.25 litres

grapefruit marmalade

3 medium grapefruit (1kg)
2 medium lemons (360g)
2.5 litres water
2.5kg sugar, approximately

1 Cut unpeeled grapefruit and lemons into thin slices, discard seeds. Combine fruit and water in large bowl; cover, stand overnight
2 Place fruit mixture in large saucepan, bring to a boil. Reduce heat; simmer, covered, for about 45 minutes or until rind is soft.
3 Measure fruit mixture, allow 1 cup (220g) sugar to each cup of fruit mixture. Return fruit mixture to pan, add sugar; stir over heat, without boiling, until sugar dissolves. Bring to boil; boil, uncovered, without stirring, for about 15 minutes or until marmalade jells when tested.
4 Pour hot marmalade into hot sterilised jars; seal while hot.

makes about 2.5 litres

chunky breakfast marmalade

4 large Seville oranges (800g)   1.5 litres water
2 medium lemons (360g)   1.5kg sugar

1 Cut unpeeled fruit into quarters, reserve centre pith. Cut each quarter into thick slices, reserve seeds. Tie reserved seeds and reserved pith in a piece of muslin. Combine fruit, muslin bag and water in large bowl, cover, stand overnight.
2 Transfer mixture to large saucepan, bring to boil, simmer, covered for 1½ hours or until rind is soft; discard bag.
3 Add sugar, stir over heat, without boiling, until sugar is dissolved. Bring to boil, boil, uncovered, without stirring, for 10 minutes or until marmalade jells when tested.
4 Pour hot marmalade into hot sterilised jars; seal while hot.

makes about 2 litres

orange & carrot marmalade

6 large oranges (1.25kg)   6 medium carrots (700g), grated
2 medium lemons (360g)   2kg sugar, approximately
1 litre water

1 Slice unpeeled fruit finely, reserve seeds and tie in a piece of muslin. Combine fruit, muslin bag and water in large saucepan. Bring to a boil, simmer, covered for about 1 hour or until rind is soft. Stir in carrots, simmer further 15 minutes.
3 Measure fruit mixture, allow ¾ cup sugar to each cup of fruit mixture. Return fruit mixture and sugar to pan, stir over heat, without boiling, until sugar is dissolved.
4 Bring to boil, boil, uncovered, without stirring. for about 20 minutes or until marmalade jells when tested.
5 Pour hot marmalade into hot sterilised jars; seal while hot.

makes about 2 litres

mandarin marmalade

12 medium mandarins (1.25kg)
1.5 litres water
1.5kg sugar, approximately
80ml lemon juice
60ml Cointreau

1 Peel mandarins, cut rind into fine strips, Remove pith and seeds from mandarins; tie seeds in a piece of muslin. Finely chop flesh. Combine rind, muslin bag, flesh and water in large bowl, cover, stand overnight.
2 Transfer mixture to large saucepan, bring to boil, simmer, covered for 30 minutes or until rind is soft; discard bag.
3 Measure fruit mixture, allow 1 cup sugar to each cup of fruit mixture. Return fruit mixture and sugar to pan, stir over heat, without boiling, until sugar is dissolved; stir in juice. Bring to boil, boil, uncovered, without stirring, for 35 minutes or until marmalade jells when tested.
4 Stir in Cointreau, stand 10 minutes before pouring hot marmalade into hot sterilised jars; seal while hot.

makes about 2 litres

glossary

almonds flat, pointy ended nuts with pitted brown shell enclosing a creamy white kernel that is covered by a brown skin.
slivered cut lengthways.

Certo commercially-made pectin product extracted from apples; used in the home jam making process. Available at supermarkets or on the Internet.
cinnamon dried inner bark of the shoots of the cinnamon tree; also available in ground form.
cloves can be used whole or in ground form. Has a strong scent and taste so should be used minimally.

cointreau citrus-flavoured liqueur.
cornflour also known as cornstarch; used as a thickening agent in cooking.
cumquat fruit resembling small, oval oranges.
figs small, soft, pear-shaped fruit with a sweet pulpy flesh full of tiny edible seeds. Vary in skin and flesh colour according to type, not ripeness; when ripe, figs should be unblemished and bursting with flavour; nectar beads at the base indicate when a fig is at its best. Figs may also be glacéd (candied), dried or canned in sugar syrup.

food colourings available in liquid, powdered and concentrated paste forms.
framboise a raspberry-flavoured liqueur; crème de framboises is sweeter.
ginger
fresh also called green or root ginger; the thick gnarled root of a tropical plant. Ginger can be stored, peeled, covered with dry sherry in a jar and refrigerated, or frozen in an airtight container.

stem fresh ginger that has been crystallised in sugar syrup.

orange, seville variety of orange that is very tart in flavour; suitable only for jam-making.

papaya also known as pawpaw;
thin-skinned tropical fruit, the ripe flesh
of which varies from orange to yellow

to pink in colour. Green pawpaw is a
popular ingredient in curries and
chutney.

passionfruit also known as granadilla;
a small tropical fruit, native to Brazil,
comprised of a tough skin surrounding
edible black sweet-sour seeds.

pecans native to the United States;
golden-brown, buttery and rich.

pine nuts also known as pignoli; small,
cream-coloured kernels obtained
from the cones of different varieties of
pine trees.

pistachios pale green, delicately
flavoured nut inside hard off-white

shells. To peel, soak shelled nuts in
boiling water about 5 minutes; drain,
then pat dry.

port sweet fortified wine with alcohol
content of 18% to 20%.

quince large, yellow-skinned, fragrant
fruit with crunchy cream flesh that,
when slow-cooked, turns a deep
ruby-red in colour.

rum liquor made from fermented
sugarcane.

sauternes a sweet white wine made
from late-harvested premium grapes;
often referred to as a botrytis or sticky
wine.

sherry sweet fortified wine originally
from the south of Spain.

sugar we used coarse, granulated
table sugar, also known as crystal
sugar, unless otherwise specified.

caster also known as superfine or
finely granulated table sugar.

whisky we used a good quality
Scotch whisky.

conversion charts

MEASURES

The cup and spoon measurements used in this book are metric: one measuring cup holds approximately 250ml; one metric tablespoon holds 20ml; one metric teaspoon holds 5ml.

All cup and spoon measurements are level.

The most accurate way of measuring dry ingredients is to weigh them. When measuring liquids, use a clear glass or plastic jug with metric markings.

We use large eggs with an average weight of 60g.

WARNING This book may contain recipes for dishes made with raw or lightly cooked eggs. These should be avoided by vulnerable people such as pregnant and nursing mothers, invalids, the elderly, babies and young children.

DRY MEASURES

METRIC	IMPERIAL
15g	½oz
30g	1oz
60g	2oz
90g	3oz
125g	4oz (¼lb)
155g	5oz
185g	6oz
220g	7oz
250g	8oz (½lb)
280g	9oz
315g	10oz
345g	11oz
375g	12oz (¾lb)
410g	13oz
440g	14oz
470g	15oz
500g	16oz (1lb)
750g	24oz (1½lb)
1kg	32oz (2lb)

LIQUID MEASURES

METRIC	IMPERIAL
30ml	1 fl oz
60ml	2 fl oz
100ml	3 fl oz
125ml	4 fl oz
150ml	5 fl oz (¼ pint/1 gill)
190ml	6 fl oz
250ml	8 fl oz
300ml	10 fl oz (½ pint)
500ml	16 fl oz
600ml	20 fl oz (1 pint)
1000ml (1 litre)	1¾ pints

LENGTH MEASURES

METRIC	IMPERIAL
3mm	⅛in
6mm	¼in
1cm	½in
2cm	¾in
2.5cm	1in
5cm	2in
6cm	2½in
8cm	3in
10cm	4in
13cm	5in
15cm	6in
18cm	7in
20cm	8in
23cm	9in
25cm	10in
28cm	11in
30cm	12in (1ft)

OVEN TEMPERATURES

These oven temperatures are only a guide for conventional ovens. For fan-assisted ovens, check the manufacturer's manual.

	°C (CELSIUS)	°F (FAHRENHEIT)	GAS MARK
Very low	120	250	½
Low	150	275–300	1–2
Moderately low	160	325	3
Moderate	180	350–375	4–5
Moderately hot	200	400	6
Hot	220	425–450	7–8
Very hot	240	475	9

index

This book is published by Octopus Publishing Group Limited based on materials licensed to it by ACP Magazines Ltd, a division of PBL Media Pty Limited
54 Park St, Sydney
GPO Box 4088, Sydney, NSW 2001
phone (02) 9282 8618;
fax (02) 9267 9438
acpbooks@acpmagazines.com.au;
www.acpbooks.com.au

OCTOPUS BOOKS
Design: Chris Bell
Food Director: Pamela Clark

Published and Distributed in the United Kingdom by Octopus Publishing Group Limited
Endeavour House
189 Shaftesbury Avenue
London WC2H 8JY
United Kingdom
phone + 44 (0) 207 632 5400;
fax + 44 (0) 207 632 5405
aww@octopusbooks.co.uk;
www.octopusbooks.co.uk
www.australian-womens-weekly.com

Printed and bound in China

International foreign language rights,
Brian Cearnes, ACP Books
bcearnes@acpmagazines.com.au

To order books:
telephone LBS on 01903 828 503
order online at
www.australian-womens-weekly.com
or www.octopusbooks.co.uk